Photo Exploration

Montserrat

& Montserratians

Commemorating Ten Years Living with the Volcano (1995-2005)

5   4   3   2   1

Published and distributed by KiMAGIC www.kimagic.com

Library and Archives Canada Cataloguing in Publication

Kravtchenko, Igor, 1965-
Montserrat and Monserratians : photo exploration : commemorating ten years living with the volcano, 1995-2005 /
Igor Kravtchenko ;
introduction by Howard A. Fergus.

ISBN 0-9736950-0-5

1. Montserrat--Pictorial works. I. Title.

F2082.K73 2005   972.97'5'00222
  C2005-904296-6

Printed and bound in Canada
Printed on acid-free paper.

Contents

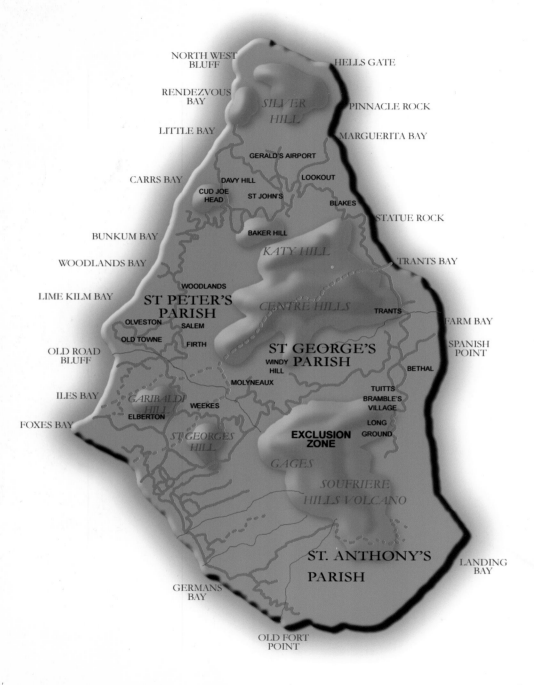

NORTH WEST
BLUFF

HELLS GATE

RENDEZVOUS
BAY

*SILVER
HILL*

PINNACLE ROCK

LITTLE BAY

MARGUERITA BAY

GERALD'S AIRPORT

CARRS BAY

DAVY HILL

LOOKOUT

CUD JOE
HEAD

ST JOHN'S

BLAKES

STATUE ROCK

BAKER HILL

BUNKUM BAY

KATY HILL

WOODLANDS BAY

TRANTS BAY

LIME KILM BAY

WOODLANDS

CENTRE HILLS

TRANTS

FARM BAY

**ST PETER'S
PARISH**

OLVESTON

SALEM

OLD TOWNE

FIRTH

**ST GEORGE'S
PARISH**

SPANISH
POINT

OLD ROAD
BLUFF

WINDY
HILL

BETHAL

MOLYNEAUX

ILES BAY

*GARIBALDI
HILL*

WEEKES

TUITTS
BRAMBLE'S
VILLAGE

ELBERTON

FOXES BAY

*ST GEORGES
HILL*

LONG
GROUND

**EXCLUSION
ZONE**

GAGES

*SOUFRIERE
HILLS VOLCANO*

**ST. ANTHONY'S
PARISH**

LANDING
BAY

GERMANS
BAY

OLD FORT
POINT

Preface from Photographer

I carried an idea of this book about Montserrat for a long time. Why Montserrat? I fell in love with this green tiny island from the first minute I saw it from the ferry.

This book includes photographs from different trips: during Christmas Festival, celebrations of St. Patrick's days in March and Queen's Parade in June. I had a chance to explore the underwater world, enjoy the tranquility and colors of the rainforest, and admire magnificent views from the hills.

Montserratians are very friendly and atmosphere of security and hospitality presents everywhere on the island.

Living with the active volcano for ten years made these people strong and able to survive in very hard situations, and they did not lose their ability to enjoy life in its simplicity.

In this book you will find a lot of photographs of local talents, some of them are well known, others are just the rising stars.

My special thanks to those who helped me with this project: Government of Montserrat, Montserrat Tourist Board, Chamber of Commerce, Development Unit, Sea Wolf Diving Centre and all those who were involved during my trips.

Igor Kravtchenko

Welcome to
Montserrat
Still home
Still nice

GOVERNMENT OF MONTSERRAT

Introduction

1   History of the Island

Montserrat is not just another British colony; it has a unique romantic story. Its first known inhabitants were the colourful Taino Indians, who settled along its coastal areas near water sites. These were followed by Irishfolk in search of peaceful shrines at which to worship, like some of the Puritans who fled from England to America in the 1620s. The Montserratian religious refugees were however Roman Catholics, and ironically, some came from Protestant America, and Virginia in particular, whose religious intolerance drove them to this small corner of the Antilles. Roman Catholic settlers came from two other sources: one was neighboring St. Kitts from which Protestant intolerance also drove them; the other was Ireland itself from which the Puritan English ruler Oliver Cromwell sent them as prisoners of war, after he had subjugated that country in a 1648 battle.

Religion and Irishness are therefore at the heart of Montserrat's early history. The major Christian denominations such as Anglican, Methodists, Pentecostals, Roman, Seventh Day Adventists are found on Montserrat. In fact it was a well-known Roman Catholic asylum, and one historian has dubbed it with doubtful veracity 'Ireland's only Colony'. It was the Irish who gave names to people, estates, villages, heights and shorelines – names such as Farrell, St. Patrick's, Riley, Cork Hill, Sweeney, Galways, Reid's Hill, Banks, Kinsale, Galloway, Irish and Fergus. It is even widely claimed by outsiders who think they know that Montserratians speak with a 'distinct brogue' and a 'lilt' that are attributed to the Irish connection. This nineteenth century story may well be apocryphal but it humorously illustrates the point:

Montserrat had Irish colonists for its early settlers and the negroes to this day have the Connaught brogue curiously engrafted on to the African jargon. It is said that a Connaught man on arriving at Montserrat, was, to his astonishment, hailed in the vernacular Irish by a Negro from one of the first boats that came alongside. 'Thunder and turf' exclaimed Pat, 'how long have you been here?' 'Three months! And so black already!' "Hanum a diaul" says Pat, thinking Quashie a country man, 'I'll not stay among ye'; and in a few hours the Connaught man was on his way, with a white skin to the Emerald Isle.

The story does not credit the Connaught man with much common sense, but it underlines the historic connection.

A 1678 census put the Irish number at 1869 in a total population of 2682 as shown below:

	Men	Women	Children	Total
English	346	175	240	761
Irish	769	410	690	1869
Scottish	33	6	13	52
Whites	1148	591	943	2682
Blacks	400	300	292	992

Total peace did not come with Irish immigration and a law had to be passed to curb inter-racial and inter-political strife among the whites. The Act was intended to restrain "several odious distinctions used by the English, Scotch and Irish reflecting on each other (English Dog, Scots Dog, Tory, Irish Dog, Cavalier, Roundhead and many other opprobrious scandalous and disgraceful terms), and therefore ordains that if any such or like reflections are used in the island by any person, stranger or foreigner, the offenders shall be prosecuted as breakers of public peace, and shall abide such fines or punishments as shall be imposed on them by the Governor and Council".

In the 1678 census, Irish people formed the majority of the population but Africans who came as slaves for sugar plantations soon overtook them. The population which the 1995 eruption has reduced to about 5,000 is predominantly black. Today the white population is very small and consists mainly of expatriates who came in the wake of a real estate and resident tourism boom, which started in the 1960s. The Irish connection is still celebrated especially on St. Patrick's Day; and the national crest depicts a woman with a cross and harp. She is Erin of Irish legend who gave Ireland its second name. Between 1903 and 1951 and as recently as 1982, the lady with the harp and cross (a symbol of the 'true' faith) was printed on Montserrat's stamps.

Speaking of migration, even before the eruption, which has become a landmark in the island's history literally and metaphorically, and the downturn in the cotton industry, there was a strong Montserratian diaspora in places like Boston, New York, Montreal, Toronto and the Caribbean. Loyalty to home burns brightly though, and they send remittances to relatives (more then than now) as well as relief through their various organisations in crisis periods and they visit occasionally, but especially at Christmas.

England now has the major concentration of overseas Montserratians. They were joined by others from the USA in 2005. Having gone there for refuge from the volcanic crisis, they have outlasted their welcome and their legal residence status, and therefore had to either repatriate or move to the UK.

Some of the public ceremonies on Montserrat would seem an anachronism since there is no longer a British Empire. One of the awards for public services is KBE, which denotes Knight Commander of the British Empire. There has been, however, strong general support for retaining these ancient orders. Couple years ago a former British Governor of Montserrat, Mr. Anthony

Longrigg could be seen decked in ceremonial dress on an evening when he officiated at an investiture. He wears a plumed helmet, which is a throw-back to the 'planter' or helmet which plantation owners wore in the tropics during the days of slavery. He has in fact donated his uniform to the national museum so this particularly relic of colonialism and plantation society has been discarded.

Following British tradition, Montserrat celebrates the Queen's official birthday in June and Remembrance Day for the two World Wars in November. The guard of honour is comprised of the Montserrat Defence Force, the Royal Montserrat Police Force, the Secondary School Cadet Corps and some other uniformed organisations. They march past the Governor and do precision drills to the tune of martial airs and music of empire. In the June celebrations, the Queen arrives symbolically and at her imagined presence, the royal standard is hoisted. People do enjoy moments of colour and pageantry and the royal connection provides this is in Montserrat, though not exclusively. People certainly enjoy the imperial honours, which are awarded in January and June, although more local honours of various kinds have been increasing and are most welcomed.

2   Politics and Economy

Today's Montserrat is a British Overseas Territory with an English Governor who is currently a woman and its democratic government on the Westminster model is elected five-yearly. The head of Government carries the title, Chief Minister who heads a cabinet of five from a parliament of nine elected members. Although it continues to be a British overseas Territory, Montserrat enjoys a large measure of internal self-government and political stability.

Montserrat, which belongs to the Leeward Islands in the Lesser Antillean chain of the Caribbean islands, can be reached through Antigua, its international gateway. It is equally near to French Guadeloupe. This beautiful island with equally beautiful people set in the azure waters of the Caribbean is a veritable haven of rest and tranquility. A helicopter and a ferry ply between Antigua and Montserrat daily but this is scheduled to change in July 2005 when construction of a new airport would have been completed.

The island has a romantic history of air transportation. The regional carrier Leeward Island Air Transport (LIAT) was actually born in Montserrat in 1956 the year of the opening of Blackburne Airport. This was preceded though by a small landing strip at Olveston in 1953 used by Frank Delisle, the founder of LIAT. In 1997, Blackburne which derived its name from a Leeward Island Governor was re-named Bramble to honour the island's first Chief Minister. Volcanic action dictated the move to Geralds at first to a helipad, and in 2005 to a landing strip for fixed wing planes. Meanwhile the Plymouth harbour had yielded to Little Bay the sea entrepôt and new proposed town.

The new airport is at the centre of economic development thinking on the island. It is expected to give a new take-off to the tourist industry and attract other businesses in July 2005. Her Royal Highness Princess Ann formally opened the new terminal building on February 2005; it was built with European funds which means British monies as well. The building is interestingly designed with its nests of triangular hip roofs at both ends. It is already in use by the public using helicopter services; it has checking in facilities, a café, duty free shop, departure and arrival lounges.

On the way to the airport one has to pass underneath the runway through a new road tunnel which is also the route to Drummonds and Parcel Piece. This tunnel is necessary to allow the runway maximum length to accommodate the Twin-Otto aircraft. At first, the small tunnel caused excitement, it being the island's first.

Montserratians know how to party but they are also a hard-working people who demonstrate uncommon resilience in the face of challenges. Many saw the devastating hurricane Hugo in 1989 as a blessing in disguise – an ill wind that brought some good. A Plymouth man was heard to say; "God bless Hugo, it brought me freedom". In a similar spirit there are concrete plans to transform ash into gold metaphorically and almost literally in that studies and schemes are afoot to build industries out of the large volumes of ash, gravel and debris which the volcano emitted. Building materials such as tiles are anticipated and the opportunities are generally tempting.

The new development is focused on the north of the island that has hatched new communities, new homes, new roads and new businesses. A new town is on the way at Little Bay aided by United Kingdom funds. An impressive Cultural Centre is already under construction as a voluntary exercise with funds raised by Britain's Sir George Martin of Beatles and music fame. This is good news for the Montserrat artistic community, and the new facility could be the centre of a renaissance of the arts. George Martin's love affair with the island began in the 1970s when he built Montserrat Air Studios at a hilltop at Waterworks with a magnificent view of mountain, sea and the verdant Belham Valley. So sophisticated was the recording equipment, that one visitor said that Martin had made a landfall into the twenty-second century. Her Royal Highness, Princess Ann visited the Cultural Centre in progress on 22 February 2005 and gave it her blessing.

With the completion of Little Bay the island will have a new capital as well as a sprawling business suburban area. The latter includes the Royal Bank of Canada, the Bank of Montserrat, The Credit Union Building, Farara Plaza, two Stationery Centres, a couple of micro Shopping Centres and the Government Headquarters complex which are all situated in the greater Brades area. A new Montserrat is growing up with the north of the island as its centre and this includes the many new houses that have sprung up. The Government has provided new housing villages in Davy Hill, Lookout and Drummonds and the people themselves through their own organisations are moulding former strangers into tightly-knit communities.

Not everything has trekked northward, however. Education is very important to Montserratians and there are three primary schools to serve the children in the northern zone. Meanwhile a new education complex has arisen in the Salem area for students at the secondary and tertiary levels. It is comprised of the Montserrat Secondary School, a brand–new Community College and the University of the West Indies School of Continuing Studies in new quarters which all happily and fortuitously nestle side by side. Not far away in Olveston an offshore Medical School is in operation making the general Salem area the education capital of the island. A National Trust which is active in heritage preservation and education is literally a stone's throw from both the Secondary School and the College, emphasizes the idea of an education centre at the edge of Salem and Olveston – names redolent of the Irish and English heritage.

A Development Unit coordinates the government programmes and provides guidance on economic plans, strategies and investor incentives. Tourism is expected to be a big earner of the future with a strong eco-dimension rooted in the new landscape which the volcano has created. The ruined town of Plymouth is already being mentioned in the same breath as Pompeii. The welcome mat is also out for investors in manufacturing.

3.   Hotels, Villas

The quality of housing on Montserrat has been second to none in the region beginning with the 1960s. The Vue Pointe, Montserrat's first luxury resort was associated with the real estate boom of the 1960s which saw the rearing of palatial buildings in the Old Towne area owned mainly by North Ameri-

cans. Built in 1961 by a prominent Montserratian family, the Osbornes, the Vue Pointe hotel with its picturesque chalets, is situated in the historical Old Towne area on a hillock overlooking Isles Bay. The Vue Pointe hotel aptly named from its view of Brandsby Pointe near the capital, Plymouth, commands a panoramic sweep of sea, hill and mountain. The hotel has conference facilities that can be also used for the performing arts. Accommodation is in cottages and rooms with private bathrooms, cable TV, telephones, ceiling fans and private balconies. There is also a fresh water swimming pool, two tennis courts, a library and a beach bar. Beside the hotel, Belham River empties into Isles Bay and the in-between-verdant valley used to be

the site of an attractive golf course that threatens to spring back to life. Vue Pointe visitors do not have to worry about leisure activities - island

singers do not hastily assemble to entertain. One group of singers was founded by scholar and musician Dr. James Irish and it features folk and other indigenous songs rooted in research and creativity. They have been singing for over 33 years, and for nearly as many at the Vue Pointe resort. They have also sung to great acclaim in the Caribbean, England and the USA. They drew commendation at the first Caribbean Festival of Arts (CARIFESTA) in Guyana in 1973 for the 'haunting quality of their lyrics'. Their enthusiasm infects and captivates the Vue Pointe audience.

The Tropical Mansion Suites is an elegant hotel built in the north of the island after the abandonment of Plymouth. A tribute to island craft and skill, it was designed, engineered, constructed and is owned by the J.E. Galloway family; it blends old and new architectural styles pleasingly. It has a strategic location, and the Hotel capitalizes on the northeast trade winds, tranquil skies and the blue of the Caribbean Sea. This hotel represents the new development thrust on the northern side of the island and an abiding faith in its future.

Montserrat is an island of villas many of which can be rented from the island's real estate agents. On Montserrat almost all villas have fresh water swimming pools and, of course, all have stunning views of sea and mountains. By renting a villa on Montserrat one can combine the benefits of a first class resort and own home, including the luxury of having trained staff and relaxing in privacy. Villa rentals and winter residential tourism in Montserrat drove the economy for decades and still do.

Dining options in Montserrat are varied and fascinating. One can choose from the snackettes and welcoming small restaurants spread around the island, bakeries or bars. Dining in balmy evenings offers a chance to be adventurous with the selection of cuisines on offer. The delight of dining is accentuated by varied and creative settings. "Ziggy's Restaurant" has unique set up in the small chalet hidden in the rainforest. Her Royal Highness Princess Ann of England is one of the many distinguished persons who have dined in this romantic setting. The night-time ambience is different from the day but the appeal is constant. There is also a number of small shops that specialize in fresh vegetables and meats, small bakeries that sell fresh bread and pastries.

4. Volcano and Nature

The eruption of the Soufriere Hills volcano in 1995, which threatened to blow Montserrat out of existence only succeeded in placing it more prominently on the map of the world. Montserrat is a volcanic island and it has unique black sand beaches, high mountains and lush vegetation. Nowhere in the world you can get this close to a volcano, which has wrought so much havoc. The stark contrast between the green and fertile Centre Hills, an ancient volcanic range, and the gray and barren flanks of the youthful volcano, covered now in rock and ash, is a wonder of nature.

The eruption started on 18 July 1995 but the first massive outburst came on 25 June 1997 and devastated extensive areas of the east of the island. This was the only fatal eruption claiming 19 lives of persons labouring on the Farrell's flank of the volcano. Yet another major dome collapse occurred on Boxing Day of the same year and yet again on 20 March 2000. The volcano has been generally quiet for over two years now.

Montserrat Tourist Board organizes special tours for visitors to the safe areas from where the volcano can clearly be seen. On one of the images, tour guide and excursionist Lenroy Daley (Slim) orientates his visitors in preparation for a tour. Taxi drivers are also very knowledgeable of island stories and the volcano has produced added hair-raising ones. Slim himself has a dramatic true story of trying to outrun a pyroclastic flow which came after him in the village of Harris.

During the daytime visitors can admire the innocent looking Soufriere Hills on a 'calm' day but from a respectful distance. During the night time one can observe the volcano in its glowing mood. This awesome beauty has inspired lyricists and poets: "Tonight Chances peak still grows/And an unholy dome still glows". The scenes that attract sightseers are produced as incendiary rocks catapulted from the volcano roll down the mountainside. Sometimes the fire is in the sky as an eruption creates electrical charges that

generate thunder and lighting. This becomes a veritable *son et lumière* staged by Gages Soufriere.

Montserrat's volcano has been a source of great hardship for the island and its people. You might have time to travel to the east, and see the destruction done to the island only airport. Pyroclastic flows sped down these north-eastern flanks in late 1997 and burnt their way through the departure lounge into the fringes of the runway. One can see isolated buildings amongst the ash and debris, which were spared from the wrath of the volcano. However, with a volcanic activity declining, the areas impacted by the eruption will become more accessible, and visitors will be able to share in the awesome power of nature and witness the natural growth of volcanic island. The MVO (Montserrat Volcano Observatory) provides advice on volcanic activity levels to the authorities and to the public.

Round-the-island boat excursions are a common recreational and educational activity. It gives a close-up view of the volcanic devastation especially on the less easily accessible southern and eastern sides. Be prepared for varied scenes including Long Ground the first village which the eruption impacted; it is now green like an oasis sandwiched in fields of ash and debris.

Volcano or not, this green mountainous island is always a big draw for nature lovers. Rain forest hiking is obviously as invigorating as it is educational and therapeutic. Amateur mountain climbing has to be a pleasant pastime in Montserrat.

Montserrat's forests are rich in coconuts. Unripe coconuts often sold at the wayside provide a refreshing drink either on its own or 'cocktailed' with gin. The ripe fruit called 'copra' when dried is eaten in a variety of ways. The fronds as well as the dried shell of the fruit can be used in craftwork so very little is discarded from this versatile plant.

The mountainous, volcanic spine of the island offers spectacular vistas, while the slopes and valleys and fertile fields display rich harvests of mango, papaya, coconut and banana. The flora and fauna of Montserrat provides a delightful experience that only an exploration of tropical nature can give. The moist, rain forest and riparian vegetation encountered along the way are home to many species of wildlife. Most of the thirty-four species of resident land birds and large numbers of migrant songbirds make the island their home. The island provides a tropical birdwatcher's paradise for the enthusiast to be delighted with. Birds such as doves, pigeons, thrashers, fly catchers and colourful humming birds are common. At least three species of humming bird are known on Montserrat. Visitors know that these birds are worth the watch.

The rocky islet Redonda seen in the distance from almost any point on Montserrat is legally owned by Antigua. But it has a romantic story which includes a line of kings complete with present pretenders to the throne Montserrat is also known for unique beaches. They all, except one – Rendezvous Bay, have glistening black sand as a feature resulting from the volcanic nature of the island. They are some of the most secluded and unspoilt beaches in the world. For swimming and sunbathing they provide the most calming experience, all without harassment, removed from the population of resorts and commercial activity.

5   Underwater

If you are a diver, you should not miss an opportunity to explore the underwater world of Montserrat. Underwater expert Wolf Krebs who used to run a diving school points out that Montserrat is one of only few places in Caribbean where hard corals are virtually free of destructive disease caused by the pollution from human's activities. Most of the diving and snorkeling is done on the West side of the island avt places where the coastline

is shallow and where beaches form, the sea floor has usually a sand bottom. Under cliffs, the sea floor is usually littered with rocks and stony ledges – here the diving is spectacular. In shallow waters one can find sponges and hard corals, brain corals, pillar corals, lots of colourful fish. This is the snorkeler's paradise and the dream of photographer.

In deeper waters, to 50 feet, where all corals grow to considerable sizes, one can find small caverns full of copper sweepers, spotted drums, and other creatures who wait out the daytime hours in the safety of their hiding places. Here one can be lucky enough to spot the resting

sea turtle. Krebs contends that instead of the volcanic activity harming the reefs they are healthier than ever. The fiery flows brought huge boulders and new substrates for reefs while the tidal waters cleansed them of the ashes. The result is a veritable underwater paradise far from the madding crowd. Columbus did not see this. Let the real discovery begin.

6   Culture & Sports

During the last quarter of the twentieth century, the island experienced a renaissance in the celebration of the Irish heritage and in 1984 St. Patrick's Day became a public holiday. The new holiday was originally associated with a slave uprising which occurred on St. Patrick's Day in 1768 and the activists who were caught and killed are hailed as martyrs by Montserratian scholars. St. Patrick's Day in Montserrat means different things to different people. There is irony in the celebrations that draw Irish visitors in these days of emphasis on roots and African heritage. They join with locals regaled in emerald green. Actually, the search for a National Dress was launched formally in July 2002. Top designers put much of effort in creating the unique Montserrat National Costume that would combine the current trends with the Irish heritage.

The first two weeks of March every year are marked by the junior sports competitions. School sports are a tradition on the island's educational and entertainment calendar. The energy and determination of young athletes bent on winning symbolize the drive and verve of a people bent on beating the odds, on making a fresh start and winning the development race inspite of the handicaps. It is the national hope that the children will transfer this prowess and resolve to the work-world.

Football is also a national sport. A fully-lived life in the north of the island necessarily meant the construction of playing fields. With the generous support of the FIFA a first-class football facility was built at Blake's in the north of the island to accommodate world-class matches. This is another powerful signal of a 'new' Montserrat on the move.

Presently Montserrat may not feature on top football rankings by world standards, but Montserratian youth at study and play are conscious investments in the future. A new play field is planned for the Little Bay town to accommodate regional and international cricket and other tournaments. Sports and culture tourism has wide possibilities in the island. Kite flying is a lost art but it is being recovered in the recent years. Traditionally it was associated with Easter, but it is now a general holiday pastime.

Montserrat has no white Christmas in any sense even if a few dream about it. It is colour and carnival and the queen of all festivals. Christmas celebrations have their historical roots in plantation society when the slaves were granted a three-day break from the continuous routine of coerced labour. They were then free to indulge in song, dance and pageantry with the accompaniment of syncopated drumming all rooted in folk religion. In the era of freedom a similar spontaneity characterized the celebration with door-to-door serenades, masquerade dancing, mummies, giant puppets (moko jumbies) concerts and house parties. In the 1960s Christmas became more organized with Trinidad carnival as the model. It is now nearly a month-long colourful extravaganza of creative arts with beauty contests, calypso competitions and street dancing (jamming) as the highlights.

There is something unique about Montserrat masquerades, although there are marked resemblances to masquerades in other islands and even to the Jamaican and Belizean Jonkonnu. Masquerades are masked dancers in colourful costume complete with bells, ribbons, small mirrors and a tall attractive headdress resembling a bishop's mitre. They use hunters or cart whips to make way for themselves, to discipline each other, and, it is alleged, to ward off evil spirits. Masquerades are, a folk ensemble rooted deeply in the African heritage. Music is provided by a fife, a big boom drum, a small kettle drum of goatskin, a shak-shak or maracas and a boom pipe emitting a 'boom' sound. Masquerades are dance using western movements like polkas and quadrilles, but to the music of African drums. Both dance and dress are highly symbolic, linking religion and history even to the point of mocking western religion and critiquing planter inhumanity. The precise meanings of the ceremonial costume are not clear, but a study of similar 'masques' and rituals in Africa suggests symbols of war, guardianship and fertility. To preserve this element of the culture young children have been introduced to the art and they perform with delight. Montserratians respond instantly to the ancestral rhythm and ritual as if it is rooted in their psyche. Now that youths engage in the dance, this rich vein of folk art and ancestral culture is certain to be preserved.

Many Montserratians are exponents of the calypso art-form and the island is fortunate to have produced one of the best in Alphonso Cassell, the Mighty Arrow of international fame. He is popularly referred to as the soca monarch of the world. The poet, musician and choreographer unite in consummate expression on an Arrow stage. Some of his songs such as "Hot Hot Hot" are sung world-wide and his classical calypsos of yesteryear which make social comment are timeless. Even before the volcano thought of erupting, he celebrated Montserratian resilience in a song, "Man mus' Live" which assumes even greater meaning with the devastation and dislocation caused by the crisis. For the present writer, this is one of his best songs.

Arrow is by no means the only accomplished calypsonian in the island. Calypso Bear, Keithroy Morson is one of the calypso kings of Montserrat. He now resides in Antigua but sometimes return to participate in the annual Christmas calypso competition, perhaps the most popular national show. Winners get fame and money and the judges had better get it right if they wish to avoid the calumny of this or that fan club. This micro-island is rich with such talent. To Rosetta West one can add names like Shirley Spycalla, Ann Marie Dewar, Camille Gerald and Randy Greenaway some of whom are legends in their own right.

Not all Montserratian beauties parade on stage but those who win the annual beauty contest wear their tiara to show that they are winners of the annual Queen Show as it is often called. Since the first one was staged in 1965, it has become an integral part of the Christmas programme. Some five girls vie for the coveted title, a trip abroad with her chaperone, a monetary prize, a shower of gifts and national recognition. A creative element (referred to as talent) – singing, dancing or monologue forms part of the competition. The beauty contest is a fusion of arts involving dress designers and makers, costume and the performance. Don't hold any other function on that night for all roads lead to the beauty contest and the judge had better pick each person's winner.

One cannot imagine Christmas celebrations without Santa. And Santa Clause is as much at home in tropical Montserrat as he is in wintry climates. It is a Christmas tradition in Montserrat to get together to sing carols and the choral counterpart is presented by Emerald Community Singers and the group, **Voices**. Led by talented artist Ann Marie Dewar,the latter like the former continually strives for excellence and achieves it. Their concerts are a popular must on the annual cultural calendar.

The inviting countenance of Montserratians is an added attraction as is their unfailing sense of humour. Their penchant for nick names is but one demonstration of this creative sense of humour: Oral history tells us that a man was named "Rainy" because he was born during a heavy rain-storm; a woman was called "Mistress Miller" because she is very fond of corn and makes a noise when eating it. 'Bus Pot' received his name after saying that 'De Goberment Depot rice swell so much dat it bus' de pot'.

Finally, Montserrat is also a land of legend.
A mermaid reportedly lives at a pond on Chances peak in the now famous or infamous Soufriere Hills, with a treasure chest at the bottom of the pond. The mermaid has somehow revealed that anyone who takes her golden comb on Easter Monday and runs to the sea and wash it will possess the treasure. There is a catch however. The seekers must outrun a diamond snake that will try to touch them. If the snake succeeds, they lose the treasure and must pass the comb back for another person. No one knows where the mermaid has gone since the eruption, but the treasure is still there and Montserrat itself is a treasure waiting to be discovered. Montserrat is a land of old and new, of heritage and hope. It has open house every day and the welcome mat is out.

Photo Exploration

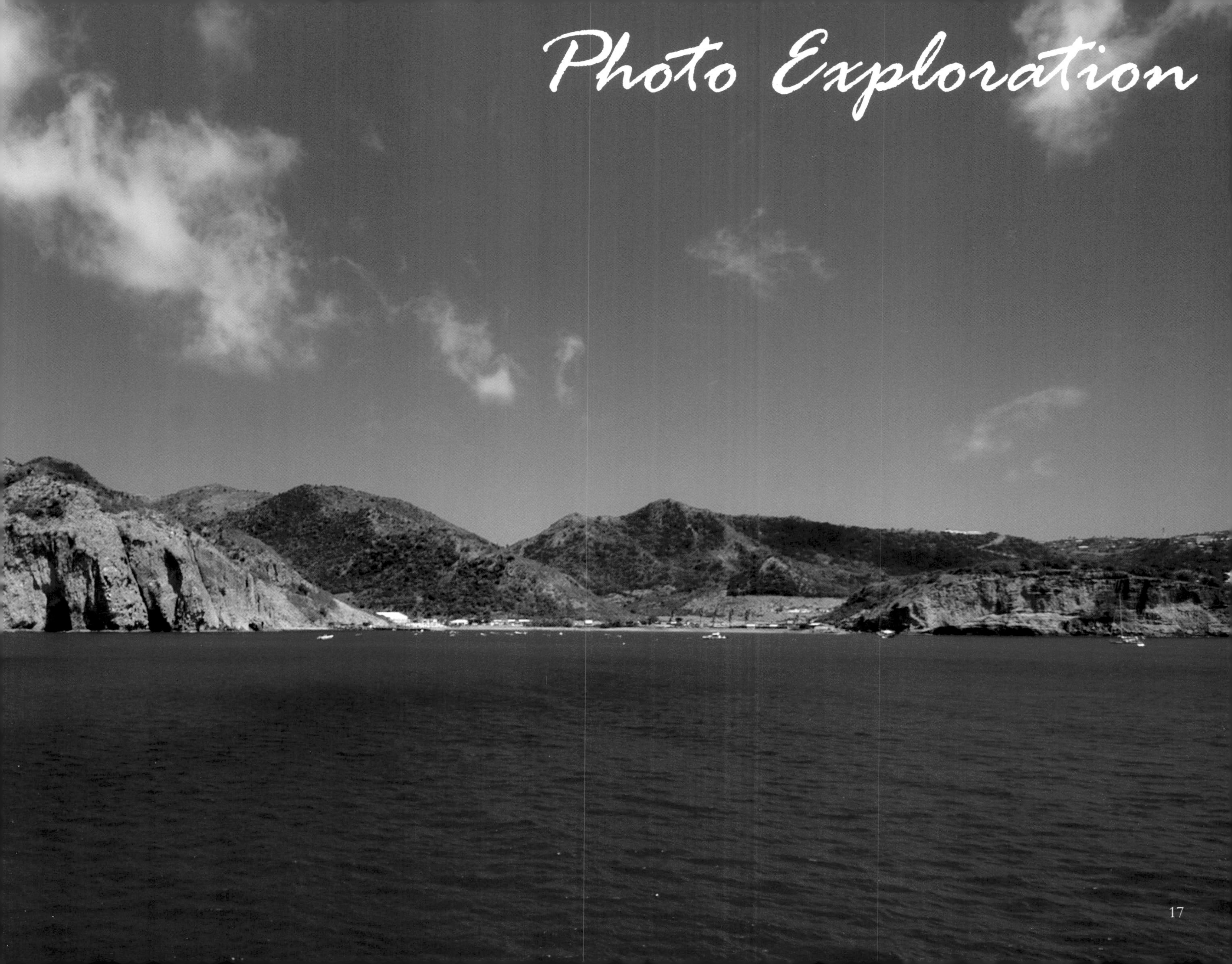

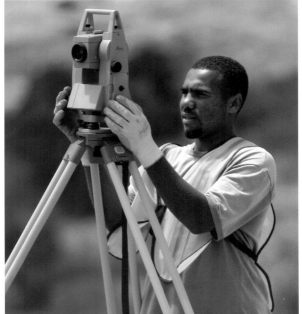

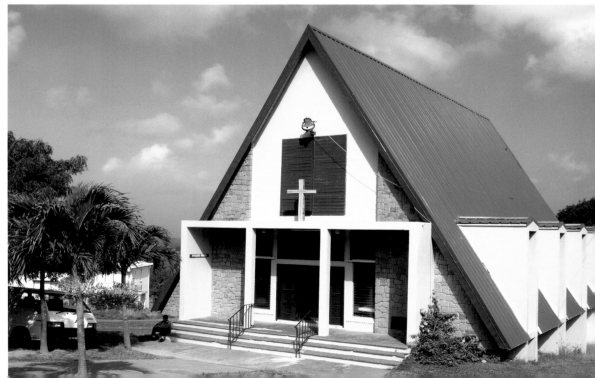

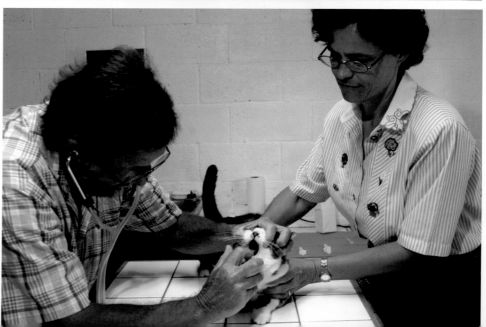

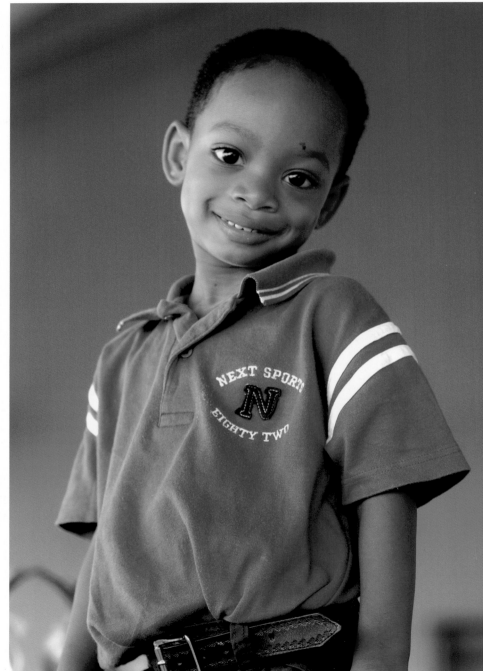

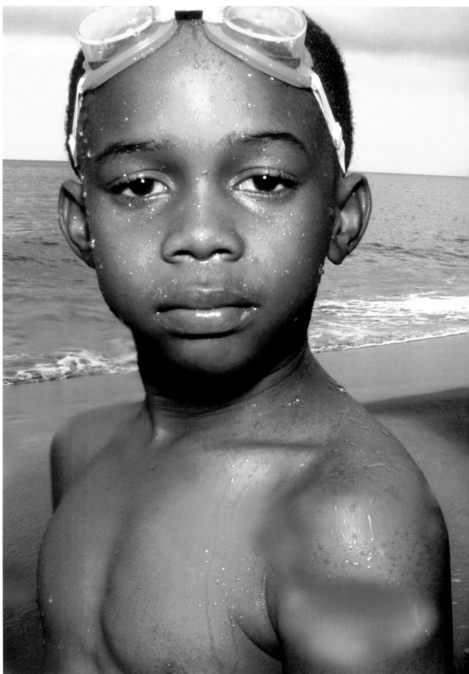

83

**"If you drink from that burn
you will surely return"**

Welcome to Montserrat
Still home Still nice

GOVERNMENT OF MONTSERRAT

About the Authors:

Igor Kravtchenko MBA, LPPO

His love to photography and passion to travel made him quit the engineering job and start own business few years ago. He developed his photographic skills through Ryerson University and Professional Photographers Association of Canada. Igor participates in numerous exhibitions and competitions in Canada and Internationally. He received the Travel Photographer of the Year 2004 award from Caribbean Tourism Organisation; Major Award of the Province of Ontario for 2004; his images were included in National Loan Collection of Canada and NAC Group International Loan Collection. Igor travelled in over twenty countries and his images were published in various travel magazines and newspapers. Montserrat became very special because of its unique nature and amazing friendliness of its people, and this book is a gift of his love to the island.

Howard A. Fergus KBE, PhD

is a Professor of Eastern Caribbean Studies, University of the West Indies, School of Continues Studies. Born in Montserrat, he was Speaker of Parliament between 1975 and 2001 and has been de facto Deputy Governor over period of nearly 30 years. Professor Fergus was knighted by Her Majesty the Queen in 2001. He has several articles in scholarly journals, book chapters and books to his credit and is also a published poet. His most recent publications are: Volcano Song. Poems of an Island in Agony (2000), History of Education in the British Leeward Islands 1838-1945 (2003), Beneath the Bananas: Poems of Montserrat (2004)